# BERNIE MADOFF

## A COMPLETE LIFE FROM BEGINNING TO THE END

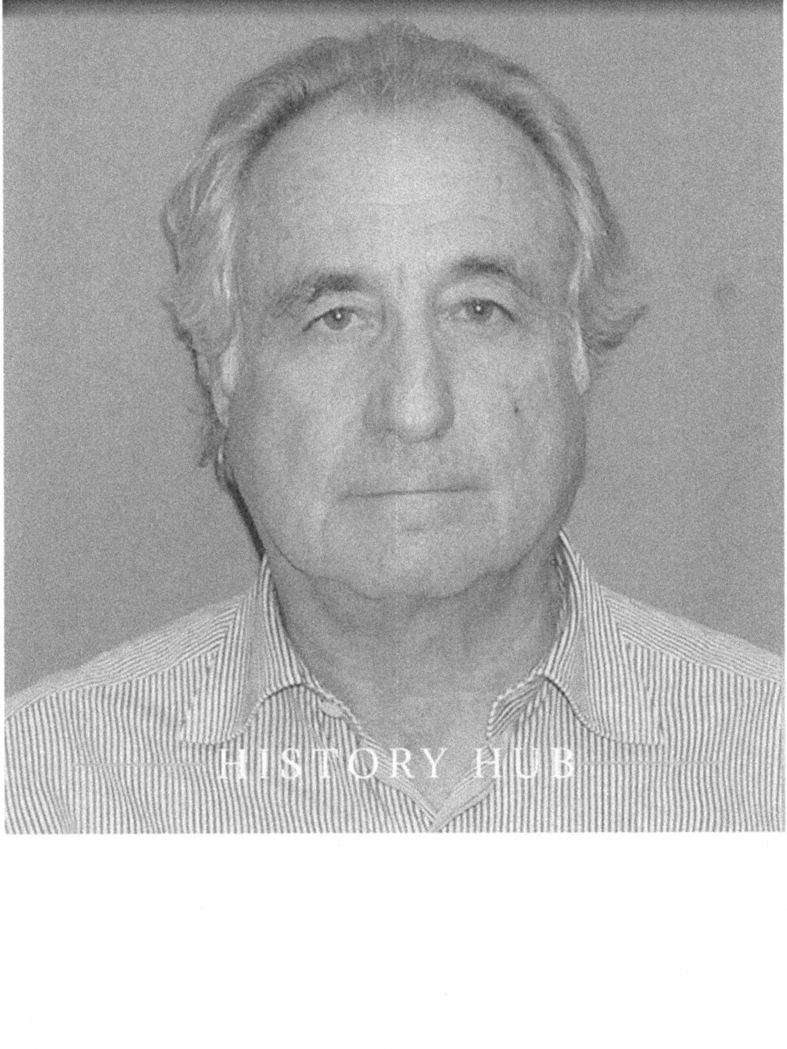

HISTORY HUB

# Bernie Madoff

## A Complete Life from Beginning to the End

*An Unauthorized Biography*

**History Hub**

# TABLE OF CONTENTS

# CHAPTER ONE
# Introduction

Bernie Madoff made it into global news for a reason he is not proud of; his name will forever be attached to the world's largest financial crime in history. However, everyone can learn a lot of lessons from his story. He managed to go through the loopholes of a financial system–that was supposedly impenetrable–that were equally abused by those before him. From another perspective, he was an extremely ambitious man who did everything he could to succeed, even to the extent of manipulating everyone around him. In doing so–in Madoff's own words–he "made wealthy people wealthier."

Bernie Madoff was an American fund manager, but his popularity transcends the world of finance. He is notoriously known for executing the largest Ponzi scheme in history, which swindled an astonishing amount of 65 million dollars from thousands of investors worldwide in a span of at least 17 years. The procedure of such a large-scale financial fraud was to pay initial investors with money acquired from later investors since actual investment income of such a business model is basically nonexistent.

Madoff's career in the stock market started in 1960 when he established a penny stock brokerage after briefly studying law the same year. He had all the support from his wife, Ruth Alpern, whom he dated since high school. Alpern's father was a retired Certified Public Accountant (CPA), whose reputation was enough to attract many investors through word of mouth. Thanks to this, the small firm grew and became the Bernard L. Madoff Investment Securities, LLC as it continued to rack up an impressive list of clientele, including celebrities such as actor Kevin Bacon and filmmaker Steven Spielberg.

As the firm grew at a staggering rate, the demand for labor and more employees prompted Madoff to employ more family members to help him. His brother, Peter Madoff, became the senior managing director and chief compliance officer in 1970, while Peter's daughter, Shana, was assigned as the rules and compliance attorney of the firm's trading division. Soon, Madoff's whole family was involved in the business, with his sons Mark and Andrew joining their father's company in 1987.

Being part of Madoff's business meant exclusive privilege—not everyone was accepted as investors, and those who were had their positive recommendations exploited to attract more people. To be admitted into Madoff Investment Securities was tantamount to having a mark of prestige, as members were not only promised higher returns, they also became part of an elite circle whose membership alone was enough to make others envious.

By the end of the 1980s, his business gained more traction for its promising annual returns of at least 10 percent—a rate not many firms could offer at the time. Madoff was so successful that his firm handled more than 5 percent of the total trading volume on the New York Stock Exchange, earning over 100 million a year. But the operations of his company were divided into two: the legitimate income-generating division and the illegitimate Ponzi scam. Most family members who worked for him claimed to have no idea about the latter, including his sons, who were responsible for exposing their father at the height of the 2008 financial crisis.

On December 10, 2008, Madoff informed his sons of his plan to give them and other higher-ups several million dollars in bonuses–months ahead of the normal payout. When Andrew and Mark asked him about the source of such a large number of funds, they were shocked by Madoff's answer-cum-confession. According to their father, the multimillion company had a branch that housed an elaborate scheme that had been operating since the 1990s. Madoff stated he would surrender himself to authorities in a week after making payments to selected employees, family members, and friends with the remaining 200-300 million dollars in cash he was left with. His sons immediately reported Madoff to federal authorities the following day, resulting in his arrest under one charge of securities fraud.

In his testimony, Madoff admitted to having lost about 50 billion dollars of his investors' money, but investigators posited that his pyramid scheme, which began as early as 1962 (debunking his 1990s claim), scammed a total of 65 billion in accounts based on the firm's financial statements. A year later, in June 2009, the 71-year-old defendant was sentenced to the maximum possible prison sentence of 150 years. Madoff pleaded guilty and emphasized that the giant scheme was only in the investment advisory division of his business and that the trading operation was legitimate. He served his sentence at Butner Federal Correctional Complex in North Carolina while authorities began the efforts of reimbursing his victims through the liquidation of Madoff's assets.

The fall of his empire haunted his business partners and investors, and some resulted in suicide and deaths. Barely two weeks after his confession, French aristocrat Thierry de la Villehuchet was trying to recover about 1.5 billion dollars in Madoff investment funds, which he procured from wealthy Europeans, including Liliane Bettencourt, the owner of L'Oreal and also the world's richest woman at the time. When all efforts were proven to be in vain, de la Villehuchet slit his wrists to atone for the sins he committed with the American fraudster. While

Madoff was serving his sentence in prison, he learned of his son Mark's suicide in 2010, who hanged himself to death out of guilt from his family's wrongdoing. Madoff's other son, Andrew, followed four years later, who died in September 2014 of lymphoma, which developed because of tremendous stress.

Madoff died on April 14, 2021, at the age of 82.

# CHAPTER TWO

## *Birth, Early Life, And Formative Years*

Bernard Lawrence Madoff, the second son of Sylvia Muntner and Ralph Madoff, was born on April 29, 1938, in Queens, New York City. His mother, who was of Romanian and Austrian descent, was a stay-at-home wife who took care of the children, while Ralph, whose parents were Polish immigrants, supported his family by working as a plumber for many years. They married each other in 1932 when the United States was in the middle of the Great Depression. Madoff had an older sister named Sondra and a younger brother named Peter.

The young Madoff attended Far Rockaway High School, where he met and fell head over heels with his future wife, Ruth. He excelled in swimming and was a member of the varsity swim team. His coach hired him as a lifeguard at the Silver Point Beach Club in a beach resort at Long Island, where he worked when there were no swimming competitions. To earn more money and to rise from the family's financial situation, Madoff had other part-time jobs, including installing irrigation sprinkler systems in various neighborhoods. After graduating from high school in 1956, he briefly attended the University of Alabama for a year and transferred to Hofstra University, where he obtained a bachelor's degree in political science in 1960. Madoff wanted to pursue a career in law and enrolled at the Brooklyn Law School, only to drop out the same year.

Madoff's father was running a store that sold sporting goods but had to close it down during the Korean War due to the steel shortage. In a phone interview from prison years later, Madoff shared how the event affected him mentally; to witness the downfall of his father, whom he greatly looked up to, was heavy on his part. He saw how Ralph dreamt of a "big business" and built it, only to lose everything instantly. The experience taught Madoff a very important lesson, and he was eagerly determined to achieve what his father did not.

After struggling for several years, the Madoffs tried their luck in the finance industry in the 1960s. Sylvia and Ralph established their own brokerage firm, the Gibraltar Securities, and registered their Queens home address as its office. But their initial endeavor in the stock market was not successful. In 1965, the Securities and Exchange Commission (SEC) ordered the firm's closure for failing to fulfill the requirements on financial reporting. It was also found that the house was under a tax lien and that the Madoffs defaulted on their outstanding obligations of more than 13,000 dollars for nine years (from 1956 to 1965). Sources close to the family suggested that the Gibraltar Securities were nothing more than a front for Ralph's under-the-table transactions.

At the same time, the 22-year-old Madoff used his 5,000 dollars savings from his past gigs and borrowed an additional 50,000 dollars from relatives and in-laws to establish the Bernard L. Madoff Investment Securities, LLC. Madoff learned many things from his parents' business, and he focused on making his own firm succeed "whatever it took." With the help and support of Ruth, who previously worked on Wall Street, and her father, accountant

Saul Alpern, who recommended the newly created investment firm to his network, the name Madoff slowly gained popularity in the stock exchange arena.

# CHAPTER THREE
# *Professional, Adult Life, and Death*

**Bernard L. Madoff Investment Securities, LLC:**

Madoff started his investment firm with the help of his family and in-laws. His goal was to earn money by matching buyers and sellers who wanted to transact penny or smaller stocks, particularly from unlisted companies that are not part of big exchanges. In essence, Madoff's company was a market maker, and in this way, small firms on Wall Street were given a chance to be competitive.

The company, which remained a sole proprietorship for 41 years before incorporating in 2001, acted as a third market trading platform that directly accepted OTC orders from retail brokers. Through this, investors did not need exchange specialist firms and would just let Madoff's company make the market for them.

**Investment Advisory:**

Official investigation based on SEC documents revealed that Madoff started managing money for clients in 1962, two years after Madoff Investment Securities was established. They are mostly accounts channeled through Saul Alpern, Ruth's father, and Frank Avellino, one of Alpern's partners, whose influence and reputation brought more clients into Madoff's firm. Among his first investors was the famous American entrepreneur and philanthropist Carl J. Shapiro, who believed in Madoff's vision and invested 100,000 dollars. Soon, Madoff was managing a multi-billion business that operated not only in the United States but also in other countries. This investment advisory division housed the largest Ponzi scheme in history that defrauded thousands of people who believed in Madoff's promise of high returns.

**NASDAQ, SEC, Government, and other Affiliations:**

Madoff's reputation in Wall Street continued to skyrocket as more investors flocked under him. Because of his expertise and tenure in the industry, he was appointed NASDAQ chairman three times–in 1990, 1991, and 1993.

At the same time, Madoff sat on a number of SEC advisory committees, including the committee on market information in October 2000, the roundtable meeting on the market structure in October 2002, and the Regulation National Market System (NMS) in April 2004.

Madoff cultivated many relationships with various government officials. He was a known supporter of the Democratic Party, where he donated 25,000 dollars every year to its senatorial campaign committee and some of its trustees. When the fraud was exposed, some of those who received donations from Madoff either returned the funds or donated a part of them to other victims. Among them was Senator Charles Schumer, who gave almost 30,000 dollars back to the trustees, and Senator Christopher Dodd, who donated 1,500 dollars to a Madoff victim foundation.

Madoff was a board director and a committee chairman of the Securities Industry Association, the predecessor of the Securities Industry and Financial Markets Association (SIFMA). He was one of the founding members of the International Securities Clearing Corporation, the London subsidiary of the Depository Trust and Clearing Corporation (DTCC). Madoff's relatives were likewise involved in these institutions, including his brother Peter, who served on SIFMA's board of directors twice, and his niece Shana, a member of the body's compliance and legal committee.

**Personal Life:**

Madoff married Ruth Alpern, whom he met at Far Rockaway High School. They married on November 28, 1959, while both were completing their bachelor's degree—at Hofstra for Madoff, and at Queens College for Ruth. They had two sons Mark, born in March 1964, and Andrew, born in 1966.

**Death:**

On April 14, 2021, Madoff succumbed to a variety of health issues, including hypertension and chronic kidney disease, while serving his 12th year in prison. Upon his death, the world reminisced about his legacy of being the world's most successful fraudster.

# CHAPTER FOUR
## *Main Difficulties in Life*

**The Investment Scandal:**

In the 1970s through the 1980s, most people in Wall Street knew Madoff's name due to the increasing popularity of his investment firm. In 1989, he was introduced to the Fairfield Greenwich Group through Jeffrey Tucker and Walter Noel, both firm partners. They entrusted 1.5 million dollars for Madoff to manage and added another five million the following year. This is just one of the many "feeder funds" that Madoff managed in the entirety of the scheme.

Soon, many hedge funds managers connected with Madoff in the hopes of benefiting from his "Midas' touch." They were easily attracted by Madoff's arrangement simply because he did not charge any fees–he earns through commissions. In 1990, investor Ezra Merkin invested a large number of assets from his hedge funds to Madoff, which the latter managed almost exclusively until his arrest in 2008. Around this time, Sandra Manzke, Tremor and MAXAM Capital hedge fund founder, invested in him as well. But Madoff told her not to divulge this connection since the investment advisory business was not officially registered with the SEC.

In his confession, Madoff stated that he never invested any of his client's money but instead deposited them into his personal bank account with JPMorgan Chase (previously Chase Manhattan Bank). He simply paid withdrawing customers out of this account since there were no actual investment gains. It was found that JPMorgan earned at least 483 million dollars from his bank account alone–the reason many believed why the bank was not compelled to investigate the billions of funds poured into it. Madoff was committed to living up to his promised high returns, and he successfully did that without making legitimate investments in a span of almost five decades.

Madoff's fraud, which has been operating for several decades, went unnoticed by government regulatory bodies.

However, not everyone was blinded by the firm's positive reputation backed by actual high returns. Harry Markopolos, a financial fraud investigator, knew something was off with Madoff's business. After his investigation, he concluded that the numbers reported by Madoff couldn't be supported or justified despite taking into consideration all aspects of the company's operations. Markopolos often informed the SEC about the fraudulent scheme, only to be ignored by their Boston office in 2000 and 2001 and by SEC New York in 2005 and 2007. Authorities continued to turn a blind eye on Madoff even after solid evidence was submitted by Markopolos. He co-wrote a book with lawyer Gaytri D. Kachroo, entitled *No One Would Listen* (2010), sharing the story of the SEC's failure to apprehend Madoff's scheme earlier on.

**Arrest and Imprisonment:**

In the first week of December 2008, Madoff struggled to pay 7 billion dollars in obligation. The challenge came along with the housing crisis, which affected most of the United States the same year. After infusing cash from various sources, including long-time investors and newly recruited members, Madoff accepted that the remaining redemption requests could not be met. He told Frank DiPascali, his assistant for over three decades, that the scheme was over–it was time to surrender. On December 9, he informed his brother Peter, and his sons Andrew and Mark about the fraud, saying that everything was "just one big lie." Madoff wanted to spend the rest of the week paying selected family members and friends with the remaining balance in his account.

However, his sons, albeit shocked with the confession, did not wait for the week to be over and immediately got in contact with federal authorities. After his arrest on December 11, Madoff posted a 10-million-dollar bail. However, he was sent to the Metropolitan Correctional Center three months later after Judge Denny Chin revoked the bail. By this time, Madoff's assets and personal properties were frozen by federal courts, and his investors were horrified by the news. At the end of the trial, Madoff was sentenced to 150 years in prison.

**Victim Compensations:**

New York lawyer Irving Picard was appointed trustee to supervise the liquidation of Madoff's assets in bankruptcy court. He also sued those who gained any profit from the Ponzi scheme. By December 2018, he reportedly recovered 13.3 billion dollars out of the 65 billion dollars defrauded. The Madoff Victim Fund (MVF) was established in 2013 to help victims claim a part of what they lost, but payouts only started in 2017 and the total amount released was only 4 billion dollars. Most claims were made by indirect investors, making the process slow and tedious as thousands of requests have to be sifted through. In November 2018, the MVF paid over 27,300 victims who received an aggregate recovery of 56.65 percent of their losses. Until now, a sheer number of Madoff investors remain unpaid.

**Deaths Linked to Madoff Ponzi Scheme:**

On the morning of Madoff's arrest's second anniversary, Mark Madoff, in an email, asked his lawyer to take care of his family and left emotional messages to his wife, Stephanie.

Moments later, he took his own life—on his second suicide attempt, the first being in 2009. Andrew Madoff, on the other hand, succumbed to cancer in September 2014. He, too, blamed his father for the relapse of the disease he previously had in 2003 and went into remission. Madoff wept in prison upon learning the news; he didn't speak or see any of his sons again since they turned him in December 2008.

His sons were not the only ones who died because of him. French hedge fund manager Rene-Thierry Magon de la Villehuchet took sleeping pills, slit his wrists, and bled to death—he invested over 1 billion dollars of his elite European clients' money with Madoff. Additionally, a handicapped British soldier named William Foxton, who after losing his life savings to Madoff, shot himself in the head upon learning of the news.

# CHAPTER FIVE
## *Main Achievements*

**Biggest Market Maker:**

Despite the events that had transpired towards the end of Madoff's life, it goes without saying that he was one of the most accomplished men on Wall Street. The empire he built from scratch, notwithstanding the implications of his illegal activities, has dominated the market for quite some time. Madoff Investment Securities, at some point, became the largest market maker in the Nasdaq Stock Market (NASDAQ). Before Madoff's downfall in 2008, his company ranked sixth among the largest market makers in the Standard and Poor's (S&P) 500 stocks.

**Electronic Trading:**

Over-the-counter (OTC) securities, the focus of Madoff's firm and whose markets were listed on the National Quotation Bureau's Pink Sheets, were less appealing than those listed on the New York Stock Exchange. To expedite the process of quoting bid and ask prices and to achieve a more efficient way of trading stocks, Madoff began using innovative computer technology at a time when the world had not yet completely grasped the advent of electronic trading. Madoff called the innovation an "artificial intelligence" capable of executing massive flow order and providing market insights. This innovation paved the way for NASDAQ, the market for electronic stocks.

**Payment For Order Flow (PFOF):**

Madoff Investment Securities was the pioneer of "payment for order flow," a practice that became more popularly known as "legal kickback." Many firms followed suit despite the criticisms and controversy, prompting the SEC to launch an in-depth investigation to rule whether PFOF was illegal or not. The commission permitted its continued practice but required brokers to disclose their arrangement with market makers.

**Exposing "Willful Blindness":**

Before Madoff's elaborate scheme was brought to the limelight, everyone thought that his offers of attractive returns were from real profits. However, most people did not believe this to be the case. Some claim that those affiliated to Madoff–his friends in the government, bank officers, hedge fund managers, and others who had business with him–knew at some point that the whole venture was "too good to be true." Madoff was earning more money at a higher rate while most firms couldn't.

In an interview with Steve Fishman, while he was in prison, Madoff posited that the system gave him the attitude of "willful blindness." Following the narrative, his downfall also exposed a system that not only enabled the scheme but profited from it. They used Madoff for their own benefit but blatantly blamed him when the scheme was caught.

As it turned out, a lot of people can prove that the attractive returns were impossible–a piece of evidence that those involved allowed the fraud to run so long as they benefit from it. Had his investment scheme been true, the overall markets would have been affected in a ripple effect; but no such thing happened—good fortune was seemingly bestowed upon Madoff only.

**Philanthropy:**

Despite his reputation as history's biggest liar, Madoff was a philanthropist who served as a board director of various nonprofit institutions. He had also made several large donations to different causes, including six million dollars to lymphoma research following his son's diagnosis of the disease and over 230,000 dollars to political programs. The Madoff Family Foundation, which Madoff co-managed with Ruth, with its many donation drives amounting to 19 million dollars, contributed to different sectors, including education, culture, and health.

# CHAPTER SIX
## *Conclusion*

There have been so many questions about Bernie Madoff, the most popular being in the lines of, "How did he manage to scam thousands of people for so long?" Some experts have diagnosed him with antisocial personality disorder, and they called him a sociopath or a psychopath. They may be correct, but great things happened, too, thanks to him and his fraud.

Madoff's case led to a paradigm shift in the regulations of the financial system. Many believed that the SEC intentionally ignored his crimes for years since they were also on the receiving end in one way or another. However, public outrage pressured the SEC to take a series of actions and changes following Madoff's arrest in 2008.

Inspections on investment advisory and brokerage firms were given heavy emphasis—protocols were revised to focus on comparative assessments of potential risks that investors may encounter. The SEC required financial companies to submit more information and strictly comply with the newly added rules. The agency's goal was to provide better asset protection against brokers and advisers to prevent theft and abuse. The SEC employed a centralized electronic system for fraud detection, which accepts tips and complaints that helps pinpoint a scheme in its early stages. The financial system saw a significant reorganization, thanks to Madoff—they finally addressed the problems and loopholes that led to the success of the Ponzi scheme.

Notwithstanding the implications of his crime, Madoff's scandal brought to light not only four decades of fraud but also the very rotten core of a system that enabled such a fraud to last for so long. He is a real-life reminder that anything "too good to be true" always has consequences, no matter what. If not for him, imagine the sheer number of Bernie Madoffs running loose in Wall Street to this very day.

The influence of Madoff's fraud case reached pop culture. His story was turned into many literary works, and some were even adapted into documentary films. In 2010, a play entitled *Imagining Madoff* portrayed Madoff's encounter with his victims; the following year, the documentary film *Chasing Madoff* was released based on Markopolos' book. The documentary miniseries *Madoff* was aired by ABC in 2016, and in May 2017, veteran actor Robert De Niro portrayed Madoff in the HBO film *The Wizard of Lies,* based on a book of the same title written by Diana Henriques.

# CHAPTER SEVEN

## Interesting Facts

## Did You Know?

Bernie Madoff was "happier in prison" than being free outside. He told Reuters that he felt safer as an inmate; for the first time in 20 years, the fear of being arrested finally left him. Madoff knew he'd die in prison, and that made him calm.

# Did You Know?

In an interview, Ruth Alpern, Madoff's wife, confessed that the couple attempted suicide on the Christmas Eve of 2008, days after their Ponzi scheme came to light. According to her, they couldn't handle what was happening, and everything was too "horrendous."

# *Did You Know?*

In July 2019, Madoff requested the Trump White House for prison sentence reduction on compassionate grounds. However, neither the former president nor any of his officials commented on the request. His lawyers filed for another injunction in February the following year, stating that Madoff was suffering from a terminal illness, only to be rejected due to the gravity of his crimes.

# Did You Know?

Madoff, who previously had billions of dollars in his bank accounts, earned 24 cents per hour after his conviction. He reportedly made 710 dollars for 3,000 hours of menial prison labor. It was reported that his performance as an aide assigned to educational programs received positive reviews from jail officers.

# CHAPTER EIGHT
## *Discussion Questions*

Madoff's grandparents from both sides were Polish immigrants. His mother was of Romanian and Austrian descent, while his father was Polish. How were immigrants treated in America during the 1930s?

# Discussion Questions

Sylvia and Ralph, Madoff's parents, started their family in 1932. What were some struggles experienced by new parents during the Great Depression? How did they differ during the 2008 economic crisis?

# Discussion Questions

Madoff was a member of the varsity team. When he wasn't competing in meets, he worked as a lifeguard in Long Island. What does this say about his skills in balancing academics, athletics, and work? How did it help him in the future? Why can't some students handle the same multitasking routine?

# Discussion Questions

Madoff idolized his father; hence, the disappointment when his business closed down. Not wanting to experience the same failure, Madoff worked hard to succeed. Do you think he would have the same drive had Ralph's business prospered? Explain.

# Discussion Questions

Madoff used his savings from previous jobs to establish his own company at 22. Do you think he was too young to lead his own firm? What did he do to compensate for the lack of academic background in finance?

# Discussion Questions

Madoff Investment Securities did not incorporate until 2001, 41 years after it was established. Which advantages of sole proprietorship did Madoff benefit from? How did the company's ownership structure contribute to the fraud?

# Discussion Questions

Back when Madoff started managing funds for his clients, investment advisory was not strictly regulated by the government. Why do you think this was the case? How did Madoff take advantage of the setup?

# Discussion Questions

Two years into the business, Madoff opened the investment advisory division of his company. How did this division benefit from the firm's main activity as a market maker? What is its role in the Ponzi scheme's success? Compare and contrast Madoff's scheme with that of the notorious Wolf of Wall Street, Jordan Belfort.

# Discussion Questions


Madoff made some donations to the Democratic Party. How did his affiliation with them affect the party's reputation after the scandal? Does it have any significant effect on their public image? Explain.

# Discussion Questions

Madoff married Ruth in 1959, while both of them were pursuing their degrees. How did his wife help him in his career? Do you think he would attain the same success if not for her?

# Discussion Questions

Several hedge funds managers entrusted their clients' money to Madoff. What are the advantages of pooled investment funds? How did Madoff take advantage of them?

# Discussion Questions

Hedge fund managers were attracted by Madoff's commission-based arrangements. Do you think the Ponzi scheme would last long had he charged fees? Why did fund managers prefer commissions?

# Discussion Questions

JPMorgan Chase reportedly earned at least 483 million dollars from Madoff's bank account. Do you agree that this was the reason for their silence for years? Would the scheme be exposed earlier had the bank investigated the funds before 2008? What was the legal basis for such an investigation?

# Discussion Questions

The SEC and other government offices did not listen to Markopolos' claims, despite the number of whistleblowing attempts. They ignored the solid proof he presented on several occasions. If you were Markopolos, what would you have done to be heard at the time?

# Discussion Questions

Madoff confessed to his sons about the scheme when he could no longer meet redemption requests amounting to 7 billion dollars. What is the role of the 2008 economic crisis in his confession? Would the fraud be exposed if there was no such event? Explain.

# Discussion Questions

Madoff Investment Securities became one of the most famous market makers on Wall Street. What made the firm rise above others in the industry? Would Madoff achieve the same level of success if he started the business now?

# Discussion Questions

Madoff pioneered the age of electronic trading in the stock exchange. What does this say about his penchant for innovation? How did it revolutionize his firm and the entire market? Do you think the use of computer information technology helped Madoff hide his illegal dealings?

# Discussion Questions

Payment for order flow is colloquially known as a "legal kickback." The SEC ruled its legality to enhance competition within the market. What are your thoughts on PFOF? Do you agree with the SEC?

# Discussion Questions

Throughout the years, Madoff worked with the biggest names and the largest institutions. However, outsiders believe that they were not completely innocent–they knew about the scheme but went along with it. When the Ponzi scheme was exposed to the public, they let him take the fall alone. How did the financial system take advantage of Madoff? Why do you think he took the blame all to himself?

# Discussion Questions

The Madoff Family Foundation made generous donations to different institutions. Why do most wealthy persons involve themselves with philanthropy and charity? Why do you think he invested in the foundation?

# **Bibliography**


- AP News, "Ponzi schemer Bernie Madoff dies in prison at 82," Michael Balsamo and Tom Hays, https://apnews.com/article/bernie-madoff-dead-9d9bd8065708384e0bf0c840bd1ae711

- Biography, "Bernie Madoff Biography," Biopgraphy.com Editors, https://www.biography.com/crime-figure/bernard-madoff

- Investopedia, "Bernie Madoff," Adam Hayes, https://www.investopedia.com/terms/b/bernard-madoff.asp

- New York Magazine, "Bernie Madoff Told the Truth About One Thing," Steve Fishman, https://nymag.com/intelligencer/2021/04/bernie-madoff-told-the-truth-about-one-thing.html

- PBS.org, "The Madoff Affair Timeline," https://www.pbs.org/wgbh/pages/frontline/madoff/cron/

- Vanity Fair, "20 YEARS AFTER I FIRST QUESTIONED BERNIE MADOFF'S SUCCESS, THE GREAT VILLAIN OF THE FINANCIAL CRISIS IS DEAD," Erin Arvedlund, https://www.vanityfair.com/news/2021/04/bernie-madoffs-success-the-great-villain-of-the-financial-crisis-is-dead

- Wikipedia, "Bernie Madoff," https://en.wikipedia.org/wiki/Bernie_Madoff

- WYFF News 4, "Five things you may not have known about Bernie Madoff's epic scam," Aaron Smith, https://www.wyff4.com/article/5-things-to-know-bernie-madoff-scam/36124939#

# Extra Final Gift to You

Dear reader,

It was my utmost privilege performing a deep dive to bringing this book for you today.

Before saying goodbye, I'd like to take opportunity to offer you one final gift. If you've enjoyed this book, may I ask for a small favor of a review?

Just a few sentences would help a lot and tell others more about this book. If you do, as a way of showing my utmost appreciation,I'll send you for FREE a most cherished and valuable gift:

## Top 7 Bestsellers Treasure Box

These are my personal bestsellers sold at bookstores valued at ~$30USD, my gift to you absolutely FREE.

**To claim your gift:**

1. Leave a review where the book was purchased

2. Send a screenshot to irvinepress@mail.com

3. Receive your gift of **Top 7 Bestsellers Treasure Box**

We've prepared the best and hope you'll find this offer exciting! Hope to see you again soon.

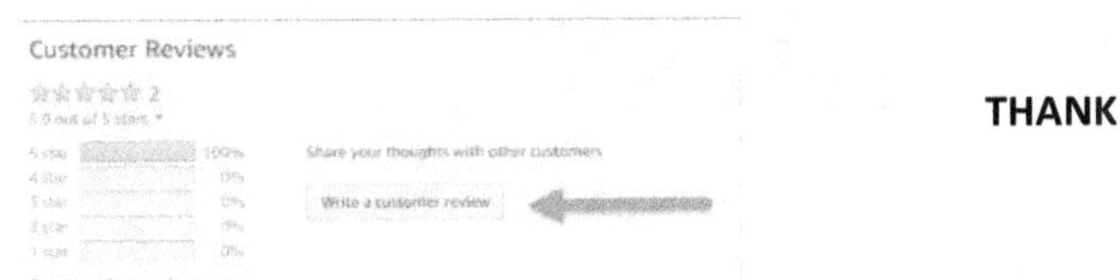

**THANK YOU**

# Don't Forget Your Free Bonus Downloads!

As our way of saying thank you, we've included in **_every_** **_purchase_** bonus gift downloads. If you've enjoyed reading this book, please consider leaving a review.

## Or Scan Your Phone to open QR code

# About Us

*"Those who don't know history are doomed to repeat it."* — Edmund Burke

More than ever, it is important that we equip ourselves with the lessons of history to ensure that we do not repeat the mistakes from the past, and learn from positive examples.

This is why History Hub exists - to provide quality history books for readers to learn important history lessons efficiently. And we'd like to make sure you learn the core lessons without the fluff. Please visit us again to access the catalog of new titles soon.

Thanks for reading,

History Hub

www.ingramcontent.com/pod-product-compliance
Lightning Source LLC
Chambersburg PA
CBHW071446150726
48000CB00006B/2459